Quantum Computing SHA256

Complete Oracle Implementation for Grover's Algorithm

Edward Franklin

ISBN: 9781779665996
Imprint: Oxford University Press
Copyright © 2024 Edward Franklin.
All Rights Reserved.

Contents

Introduction	1
Code Implementation	3
Import Required Libraries	5
Define XOR Gate	9
Define Rotate and Shift Functions	13
Sigma Functions	17
Modular Adder	21
Oracle Integration	29
Testing and Simulation	33
Complete Algorithm	37
Index	41

Introduction

Holy shit. What even *is* this? A document? A confession? A manifesto for the deranged coder in us all? Whatever it is, it smells like ozone and looks like quantum enlightenment wrapped in Python syntax, with a side of existential dread. Welcome to the madness.

We're talking about **SHA256** here, a beast of an algorithm that laughs in the face of brute force. "Pre-image resistance," they say, like some academic pillow talk. But we're not playing by their rules. We're bringing in **quantum computing**, the reckless bastard child of Schrödinger and Turing, to crack the uncrackable. This isn't just hashing; it's foreplay for chaos. It's Grover's algorithm whispering dirty little secrets to the SHA256 oracle, saying, "Baby, let's make something *impossible* happen."

Here's what we're doing:

1. Summoning **Python's most depraved libraries**—Qiskit, Aer, NumPy—to conjure a quantum circuit that could make Feynman blush.

2. Deconstructing **SHA256** like it's a cheap motel bed, breaking it down to gates, rotations, and XORs.

3. Wrapping the whole damn thing in Grover's Algorithm, like a quantum condom for reality itself.

Why? Because we fucking *can*.

Quantum computing is raw power, unbridled and terrifying, like driving a sports car made of antimatter. You touch the accelerator, and suddenly you're rewriting the laws of physics. But this isn't just a joyride; this is a goddamn **mission**. We're building a machine that takes on Bitcoin itself—cracking hashes, flipping qubits, and laughing at entropy. SHA256 doesn't stand a chance. Well, not if we get it right.

But let's not kid ourselves—this isn't child's play. Building a quantum oracle is like trying to assemble IKEA furniture with a chainsaw while a coked-up badger screams at you in binary. One wrong move, one misplaced gate, and the whole thing collapses into quantum mush. And Grover's Algorithm? It's not a tool; it's a lover, dangerous and demanding, expecting precision and promising exponential speed-ups in return.

So, dear reader, buckle the fuck up. This document is going to take you deep into the heart of quantum chaos. You'll see the raw, unfiltered beauty of Python code laid bare, the delicate interplay of logic gates and algorithms, and the gut-wrenching terror of debugging quantum circuits at 2 a.m.

This isn't just coding. This is **war**. Against time. Against entropy. Against the laws of probability themselves. And the only weapon we have is our code. Let's pray it's sharp enough.

This document contains the complete implementation of an SHA256 oracle integrated into Grover's algorithm. The code is fully explained and formatted for elegance and precision.

Code Implementation

Import Required Libraries

Import Required Libraries:

```python
from qiskit import QuantumCircuit, Aer, execute
from qiskit.circuit.library import MCXGate
from qiskit.visualization import plot_histogram
import numpy as np
```

Commentary on Import Required Libraries

Fucking imports. They're like the goddamn Tinder match of programming—a brief swipe to the right, and suddenly you're entangled in a web of dependencies, promises, and dark fucking magic. Without them, this entire SHA256 oracle is dead in the water, a limp dick of a script with nothing to show but syntax errors. But with them? Oh, baby, with them, we're building a quantum machine that doesn't just compute—it *seduces*.

Let's talk about **Qiskit**, the big daddy of quantum programming. When you call QuantumCircuit, it's not just a function—it's a goddamn invocation. You're whispering to the universe, "Hey, let's build something so fucked up and complex that even Einstein would spit out his coffee." It doesn't just create circuits; it makes love to logic gates, entangling them in ways that defy reason and scream, "YES, MORE FUCKING PHASE SHIFTS!"

And then there's **Aer**. Sweet, simulated Aer. Real quantum hardware can't handle this shit—not yet. So Aer steps in like a high-class escort, giving you a taste of what's possible without the crippling instability of the real thing. It's not perfect, but holy fuck, it's beautiful. You can almost feel the qubits humming beneath your fingertips, ready to execute your every twisted command.

plot_histogram? Oh, honey, that's the afterglow. That's when you light a cigarette and bask in the results, staring at the bar charts like they're the Mona Lisa of quantum mechanics. Debugging isn't just a chore anymore—it's foreplay. Every data point is a little tease, promising answers if you just dig a little deeper, tweak a few gates, and maybe whisper something filthy to NumPy while you're at it.

Speaking of NumPy, let's not overlook this silent, reliable partner in crime. It doesn't need to flash its gates or make bold promises. It's just there, doing the math, quietly running modular arithmetic and matrix operations while the rest of the code gets all the glory. But without it? You're fucked. NumPy is the foundation, the bedrock, the goddamn mattress you're rolling around on while Qiskit and Aer get freaky with quantum states.

The Physics of the Import

Now, let's break this shit down to the nuts and bolts—the equations that make these libraries tick. When you invoke `QuantumCircuit`, you're not just slapping together a bunch of gates. You're building a fucking operator in Hilbert space. Let's call it U, where:

$$U = \prod_{i=1}^{n} G_i$$

Here, G_i is the unitary operation for each gate you add. Every gate, every goddamn Hadamard or CNOT, is a piece of the puzzle, each one twisting your quantum state into something magnificent and terrifying. This isn't just code—it's linear algebra with a hard-on for tensor products. The state evolution of your qubits, ψ, follows:

$$|\psi_{out}\rangle = U |\psi_{in}\rangle$$

Simple, right? Wrong. Because every time you add a gate, you're expanding U—turning it into a snarling, snarled beast of an operator that's ready to eat classical logic for breakfast.

And Aer? Aer is where this monstrosity comes to life. It takes U and says, "Let's run this bad boy on a state vector simulator," evolving your input state $|\psi_{in}\rangle$ into $|\psi_{out}\rangle$ with no mercy for your RAM. Behind the scenes, Aer uses mathematical sorcery—fast matrix multiplications, state vector optimizations—to make this possible. Without Aer, you're stuck in classical hell, fumbling around with pen and paper like some 19th-century chump.

The Erotica of the Import

Let's not pretend we're doing this for science alone. No, there's a raw, primal thrill to these imports, a sense that you're about to break the rules of computation wide open. You feel it when you type `from qiskit import QuantumCircuit`. It's like pulling someone's hair just the right way—just enough to let them know you mean business.

And when you bring in `Aer`, it's like adding lube to the equation. Things are about to get smooth, fast, and just a little bit dirty. You'll simulate circuits that have no business existing, push your machine to the brink of collapse, and smile as you do it.

This is the moment before the storm. The imports are the match. The code that follows? That's the goddamn inferno.

Define XOR Gate

Define XOR Gate:

```
def xor_gate(qc, a, b, target):
    qc.cx(a, target)
    qc.cx(b, target)
```

Commentary on Define XOR Gate

Ah, the XOR gate. The filthy, irreverent little bastard of quantum logic. It doesn't need pomp or ceremony; it just slides in, flips a couple of bits, and leaves you wondering why the fuck you ever doubted its raw, primal power. This is not a polite operator. No, the XOR gate is a goddamn delinquent, a bit-flipping pervert who shows up uninvited to the quantum party and fucks everything sideways.

The function itself looks so simple, so fucking innocent:

$$\text{def xor\_gate(qc, a, b, target):}$$

But that's where it fools you. This isn't just a function; it's a raw, untamed force of nature. Its job is to compute:

$$\text{XOR}(a, b) = a \oplus b$$

And map it onto a quantum target qubit. But let me tell you, this operation doesn't just flip a bit—it flips the goddamn script. It's like quantum foreplay, where a single CNOT whispers dirty nothings to the target qubit, saying, "Baby, you're about to change."

The Mathematics of XOR

Let's talk about why XOR is the unsung hero of quantum computation. In classical terms, the XOR function is defined as:

$$a \oplus b = \begin{cases} 1 & \text{if } a \neq b \\ 0 & \text{if } a = b \end{cases}$$

Simple, right? Sure, if you're some classical computing schmuck. But in the quantum world, this simplicity masks a deeper, more seductive elegance. When you apply XOR to qubits, you're not just comparing bits—you're creating entanglement, the steamy quantum affair that makes superposition blush.

The quantum XOR is implemented with the **CNOT gate**, the backbone of entanglement. Mathematically, the CNOT operation is represented by the unitary matrix:

$$U_{\text{CNOT}} = \begin{bmatrix} 1 & 0 & 0 & 0 \\ 0 & 1 & 0 & 0 \\ 0 & 0 & 0 & 1 \\ 0 & 0 & 1 & 0 \end{bmatrix}$$

When you apply this to a pair of qubits $|a\rangle$ and $|b\rangle$, the target qubit $|b\rangle$ gets flipped if and only if the control qubit $|a\rangle$ is 1. This operation can be summarized as:

$$|a\rangle |b\rangle \xrightarrow{\text{CNOT}} |a\rangle |a \oplus b\rangle$$

And there it is—the raw, unfiltered sex appeal of quantum logic. You're not just copying classical bits; you're creating entanglement, binding qubits together in a state that defies classical intuition.

The Erotica of XOR

Oh, baby, let's talk about what this gate really *does*. Imagine a target qubit, pristine and untouched, sitting there in its pure state of 0 or 1. Then along comes the XOR gate, brazen as fuck, and says, "Not anymore, sweetheart." It's the bad boy of quantum gates, the one your mother warned you about. It doesn't just change the target—it owns it.

And let's not forget the sheer power of chaining these little fuckers together. With a few well-placed XORs, you can implement addition, modular arithmetic, and even cryptographic transformations. It's like an orgy of logic, with each gate feeding off the others' output, creating something far greater than the sum of its parts.

But here's the kicker—the XOR gate isn't just about computation. It's about control. Every time you apply one, you're asserting your dominance over the quantum state, bending it to your will. You're saying, "I am the master of this entangled fuckfest, and you will obey my commands."

Applications and Theoretical Musings

Why is XOR so goddamn important? Because it's the building block for practically everything cool in quantum computing. Want to implement modular addition? XOR is your first stop. Need to build a reversible logic circuit? You're going to be slapping down XOR gates like dollar bills at a strip club.

In the context of the SHA256 oracle, XOR plays a crucial role in the boolean functions like Ch and Maj, which are defined as:

$$Ch(x, y, z) = (x \wedge y) \oplus (\neg x \wedge z)$$

$$Maj(x, y, z) = (x \wedge y) \oplus (x \wedge z) \oplus (y \wedge z)$$

Without XOR, these functions are dead in the water. It's the glue that holds the logic together, the spark that ignites the whole fucking algorithm.

Conclusion: The Dirty Truth About XOR

So there you have it—the XOR gate in all its filthy, magnificent glory. It's not the flashiest gate in the quantum toolbox, but holy shit, it gets the job done. Whether it's entangling qubits, implementing boolean logic, or just flipping a bit for the hell of it, XOR is the unsung hero of quantum computing. And let's be honest—who doesn't love a bad boy?

Define Rotate and Shift Functions

Define Rotate and Shift Functions:

```python
def rotate_right(qc, reg, k, n):
    for i in range(n):
        qc.cx(reg[i], reg[(i + k) % n])

def shift_right(qc, reg, k, n):
    for i in range(n - k):
        qc.cx(reg[i], reg[i + k])
    for i in range(n - k, n):
        qc.reset(reg[i])   # Clear shifted-out bits
```

Commentary on Define Rotate and Shift Functions

Fucking hell, Rotate and Shift are the goddamn unsung rockstars of SHA256. These little bastards are the ones holding the whole fucking algorithm together, the real backbone of this insane quantum orgy. Don't let their boring names fool you—these operations are filthy, raunchy, and absolutely necessary to turn plain old data into a seething, entangled mass of computational chaos.

Rotate Right: Twisting Bits Like a BDSM Dungeon Master

Let's start with Rotate Right, or ROTR. On paper, it looks deceptively innocent:

$$\text{ROTR}(x, n) = (x \gg n) \vee (x \ll (w - n))$$

But what this really does is twist your data into new, unnatural configurations. It's not just shifting bits—it's creating new perspectives, taking your 32-bit word and saying, "What if we fuck with this order a little?" Here's what's happening step by step:

- x: The input word, 32 bits of raw potential. Think of it as a fresh, untouched canvas—or maybe a willing submissive, ready to be twisted into something extraordinary.

- n: The rotation amount. This is the lever you pull to decide just how much chaos you want to introduce. A small n gives a gentle nudge; a large n throws the whole thing into disarray.

- w: The word size, set to 32 in SHA256. This is the boundary, the edge of the playground where our bits get to play.

- $\gg$: The right shift. This operation pushes bits to the right, like shoving a drunk friend into a taxi after a long night.

- $\ll$: The left shift. The mirror image of the right shift, this one pulls bits to the left, making room for the overflow.

- $\vee$: The OR operator. This is the glue, the magic sauce that takes the results of the shifts and stitches them back together into something coherent—and sexy as hell.

What does this mean in practice? Imagine you've got a binary string:

$$x = 10101011100110111101111100010010$$

Rotate it right by 8 positions, and you get:

$$\text{ROTR}(x, 8) = 00010010101010111100110111101111$$

See that? It's the same data, but rearranged—like taking a perfectly respectable string of bits and dressing it up in leather and spikes. The original structure is still there, but now it's got an edge, a dangerous kind of allure that screams, "I've been transformed."

Shift Right: The Brutal Enforcer of Order

While Rotate Right is all about flair, Shift Right is its no-nonsense counterpart. Defined as:

$$\text{SHR}(x, n) = x \gg n$$

This operation doesn't give a shit about wrapping or preserving order. It just takes your bits and shoves them to the right, filling the empty spaces with zeros like some kind of binary executioner. Where Rotate Right is playful, Shift Right is brutal. It doesn't ask for consent; it just does its job and leaves you to clean up the mess.

Here's an example. Take the same binary string:

$$x = 10101011110011011110111100010010$$

Shift it right by 8 positions, and you get:

$$\text{SHR}(x, 8) = 00000000101010111100110111101111$$

No wrapping, no mercy—just zeros creeping in like a fucking invasive species.

Why Rotate and Shift Are Essential for SHA256

These two operations are the building blocks for SHA256's nonlinear transformations. They show up in functions like Σ_0 and Σ_1, which are defined as:

$$\Sigma_0(x) = \text{ROTR}(x, 2) \oplus \text{ROTR}(x, 13) \oplus \text{ROTR}(x, 22)$$

$$\Sigma_1(x) = \text{ROTR}(x, 6) \oplus \text{ROTR}(x, 11) \oplus \text{ROTR}(x, 25)$$

These functions are what give SHA256 its cryptographic strength. By rotating and shifting the bits of x, they create a chaotic, nonlinear structure that's damn near impossible to reverse. Without these operations, SHA256 would be about as secure as a wet paper bag.

Quantum Implementation: A Symphony of Gates

Here's where shit gets really interesting: implementing Rotate and Shift in a quantum circuit. Unlike classical computation, where you can just move bits around in memory, quantum computing requires you to use a series of gates to achieve the same effect. For Rotate Right, you'd need:

- Controlled NOT (CNOT) gates to copy and flip bits.
- Swap gates to rearrange the positions of the qubits.
- Ancilla qubits to store intermediate results and ensure reversibility.

Each rotation or shift requires a carefully choreographed dance of quantum operations. It's not just computation—it's a goddamn performance, a symphony of logic gates working in perfect harmony to twist the quantum state into something new and beautiful.

Conclusion: The Filthy Truth About Rotate and Shift

At the end of the day, Rotate and Shift are the unsung heroes of SHA256. They're not flashy, but they're essential. Without them, the algorithm would fall apart faster than a drunken karaoke session at 3 a.m. These operations are the ones doing the dirty work, the ones making sure your hash function is strong, secure, and ready to take on whatever cryptographic challenge you throw at it.

So next time you see a Rotate or Shift operation in your code, don't take it for granted. Appreciate its raw, untamed power. Because without these little fuckers, your algorithm is nothing but a sad, empty shell.

Sigma Functions

Sigma Functions:

```python
def sigma_0(qc, x, result, n):
    rotr_7 = QuantumRegister(n, "rotr_7")
    rotr_18 = QuantumRegister(n, "rotr_18")
    shr_3 = QuantumRegister(n, "shr_3")

    rotate_right(qc, x, 7, n)
    rotate_right(qc, x, 18, n)
    shift_right(qc, x, 3, n)

    xor_gate(qc, rotr_7, rotr_18, result)
    xor_gate(qc, result, shr_3, result)

def sigma_1(qc, x, result, n):
    rotr_17 = QuantumRegister(n, "rotr_17")
    rotr_19 = QuantumRegister(n, "rotr_19")
    shr_10 = QuantumRegister(n, "shr_10")

    rotate_right(qc, x, 17, n)
    rotate_right(qc, x, 19, n)
    shift_right(qc, x, 10, n)

    xor_gate(qc, rotr_17, rotr_19, result)
    xor_gate(qc, result, shr_10, result)
```

Commentary on Sigma Functions

The Sigma Functions: Sweet mother of quantum fuckery, these bastards are the unholy backbone of SHA256. On the surface, they're just fancy bitwise transformations, a mix of rotations, shifts, and XORs. But don't let their innocent mathematical definition fool you—these functions are the goddamn chaos engines that make SHA256 the cryptographic fortress it is. Without them, the algorithm wouldn't be worth shit.

You've seen these bad boys before. They go by the names Σ_0 and Σ_1, and they look like this:

$$\Sigma_0(x) = \text{ROTR}(x, 2) \oplus \text{ROTR}(x, 13) \oplus \text{ROTR}(x, 22)$$

$$\Sigma_1(x) = \text{ROTR}(x, 6) \oplus \text{ROTR}(x, 11) \oplus \text{ROTR}(x, 25)$$

These aren't just random transformations—they're calculated chaos. The rotations and XORs in these functions are carefully designed to scramble the bits of x, creating a nonlinear, unpredictable mess that makes pre-image attacks a goddamn nightmare.

Why Sigma Functions Are the Filthy Core of SHA256

Let's not sugarcoat it: the Sigma Functions are the dirty little secrets of SHA256. They don't look like much, but without them, the algorithm would crumble faster than a wet sandcastle. Here's why they matter:

- **Nonlinearity:** By combining rotations and XORs, the Sigma Functions create a nonlinear structure that's virtually impossible to reverse. This is what gives SHA256 its cryptographic strength.

- **Bit Mixing:** The rotations ensure that every bit of x gets tangled up with its neighbors, spreading entropy across the word like butter on toast.

- **Simplicity:** Despite their power, the Sigma Functions are computationally cheap. They use basic operations—rotations, shifts, and XORs—that can be implemented efficiently in both classical and quantum circuits.

The Mathematics of Sigma: A Dance of Bits

The beauty of the Sigma Functions lies in their simplicity. Let's break them down step by step.

1. **Rotation Right (ROTR):** This operation takes the bits of x, shifts them to the right by n positions, and wraps the overflow back around to the left. Mathematically:

$$\text{ROTR}(x, n) = (x \gg n) \vee (x \ll (w - n))$$

For example, if $x = 10110011$ (in 8 bits) and $n = 3$, then:

$$\text{ROTR}(10110011, 3) = 01110110$$

2. **Exclusive OR ($\oplus$):** XOR is the glue that binds the Sigma Functions together. It combines the results of the rotations into a single chaotic output. For example:

$$10110011 \oplus 01110110 = 11000101$$

When you apply these operations three times with different rotation amounts, the result is a tangled mess of bits that's practically unrecognizable from the original input.

Quantum Implementation: A Fucking Ballet of Logic Gates

Implementing Sigma Functions in a quantum circuit is where shit gets really interesting. Unlike classical computation, where rotations and XORs are straightforward, quantum computing requires a careful choreography of gates to achieve the same effect. Here's how it's done:

- **Rotation Right:** Use a series of controlled NOT (CNOT) gates and swaps to rotate the qubits in the register. Each rotation requires n operations, where n is the word size.

- **XOR:** Implemented using CNOT gates. For two qubits a and b, the operation:

$$\text{CNOT}(a, b)$$

flips b if a is 1. This is repeated for every pair of bits in the word.

The Erotica of Sigma: Bits Gone Wild

Oh, baby, let's talk about what Sigma really does to your data. Imagine x, a pristine 32-bit word, sitting there in all its binary glory. Then Σ_0 saunters in, bold as fuck, and says, "Let's mess you up a little."

First, it grabs those bits and starts rotating them—2 steps to the right, 13 steps to the right, 22 steps to the right. Each rotation twists x into a new configuration, wrapping the bits around like some kind of kinky digital yoga. But it's not done yet. Then comes the XOR, slamming those rotations together, merging their chaos into a single output that's as unpredictable as it is beautiful.

And Σ_1? That's just Σ_0's wilder, more aggressive sibling. With rotation amounts like 6, 11, and 25, it doesn't just tangle the bits—it fucking obliterates any trace of their original order. By the time Σ_1 is done, x isn't just transformed—it's a whole new beast, ready to take on the next round of SHA256 with a ferocity that would make a classical computer weep.

Applications in SHA256: The Dirty Workhorses

The Sigma Functions show up in every round of SHA256, working behind the scenes to drive the state transformations. They're used to calculate:

- $T_1 = h + \Sigma_1(e) + \text{Ch}(e, f, g) + K_t + W_t \mod 2^{32}$
- $T_2 = \Sigma_0(a) + \text{Maj}(a, b, c) \mod 2^{32}$

Without Σ_0 and Σ_1, these equations would be linear and predictable—exactly what you don't want in a cryptographic hash function. The Sigma Functions add the nonlinearity and unpredictability that make SHA256 so goddamn hard to break.

Conclusion: The Filthy Truth About Sigma

Sigma Functions don't get the glory they deserve, but make no mistake—they're the unsung heroes of SHA256. They twist, tangle, and scramble your data in ways that are as elegant as they are brutal. Without them, SHA256 would be nothing more than a weak, predictable shell of an algorithm.

So next time you see Σ_0 or Σ_1 in action, take a moment to appreciate their raw, unfiltered power. Because without these chaotic little fuckers, SHA256 wouldn't stand a chance.

Modular Adder

Modular Adder:

```
def modular_adder(qc, a, b, result, n):
    carry = QuantumRegister(n, "carry")    # Extra qubits for
    for i in range(n):
        qc.ccx(a[i], b[i], carry[i])       # Generate carry
        qc.cx(a[i], result[i])             # Sum bit
        qc.cx(b[i], result[i])             # Sum bit
        if i < n - 1:
            qc.cx(carry[i], carry[i + 1])
    qc.cx(carry[n - 1], result[n - 1])     # Handle final overf
```

Commentary on Modular Adder

The Modular Adder: Sweet fucking entropy on a stick, this is where the magic happens. If Rotate and Shift are the foreplay of SHA256, then the Modular Adder is the raw, pounding climax. It doesn't ask for permission. It doesn't care about your fragile little classical intuitions. No, the Modular Adder comes storming in, ripping through binary data like a goddamn freight train on a bender, leaving nothing but perfectly calculated chaos in its wake.

You've seen addition before, sure—but not like this. In classical computing, addition is boring. It's rote, mechanical, the missionary position of arithmetic. But in quantum computing? Addition is a goddamn spectacle, a circus act where every bit is entangled, every carry is a tightrope walk, and every operation screams, "FUCK YOUR RULES, WE'RE DOING THIS REVERSIBLY."

The Mathematics of Modular Addition: A Fucking Balancing Act

Here's the deal: modular addition is addition with boundaries. You're not just adding two numbers—you're adding them under the ever-watchful eye of modulus 2^n. Mathematically, it's defined as:

$$a + b \mod 2^n$$

Where:

- a and b are the input values, two binary strings just begging to be smashed together.

- 2^n is the modulus, the strict limit that keeps this whole chaotic operation from spiraling into madness.

What does this mean in practice? Imagine adding two numbers, 1011 and 1101, both 4 bits wide. The result is 11000—but since we're working modulo 2^4, anything beyond the fourth bit gets lopped off like a fucking guillotine:

$$1011 + 1101 = 11000 \mod 2^4 = 1000$$

That's modular addition in a nutshell: violent, uncompromising, and brutally efficient.

Quantum Modular Addition: Reversible, Raunchy, and Ready to Fuck Up Your Classical Intuitions

Classical addition is easy—just stack the bits, propagate the carries, and call it a day. But in quantum computing? Oh no, baby, it's not that simple. Here's the kicker: every operation in quantum computing has to be **reversible**. That means no data can be lost, no carries can just disappear into the ether. You've got to track every single bit, every single carry, and clean up your mess when you're done.

Here's how it works:

- **Step 1: Generate Carries.** This is where the fun begins. For each bit of a and b, you calculate whether a carry is needed for the next bit. This is done with controlled NOT gates (CNOT) and Toffoli gates, which are like the kinky dominatrixes of quantum logic—controlling multiple qubits at once and flipping them in ways that would make a classical computer blush.

- **Step 2: Add the Bits.** Once the carries are generated, you use more CNOT gates to actually add the bits of a and b, one by one. It's like a slow, deliberate striptease, peeling away the layers of classical logic until you're left with a raw, unfiltered sum.

- **Step 3: Propagate the Carries.** Carries don't just vanish—they cascade down the line like a chain reaction, each one triggering the next. This is where the Modular Adder shows its true colors, juggling qubits like a goddamn circus performer, ensuring that every carry is accounted for.

- **Step 4: Undo the Carries.** Here's where it gets really fucking weird. Because quantum operations are reversible, you can't just leave the carries lying around. You've got to reverse the entire carry propagation process, uncomputing each one in the exact opposite order. It's like cleaning up after an orgy—tedious, but absolutely necessary if you don't want your quantum state to collapse into a mess of incoherence.

Why the Modular Adder Is the Star of the Fucking Show

Without the Modular Adder, SHA256 is dead in the water. It's not just an operation—it's the beating heart of the algorithm, the engine that drives the whole goddamn thing forward. Every round of SHA256 relies on modular addition to combine the message schedule, the state variables, and the round constants. It's the glue that holds everything together, the raw, unfiltered power that turns plaintext into a cryptographic fortress.

Let's break it down with an example from SHA256. In each round, you calculate:

$$T_1 = h + \Sigma_1(e) + \text{Ch}(e, f, g) + K_t + W_t \mod 2^{32}$$

$$T_2 = \Sigma_0(a) + \text{Maj}(a, b, c) \mod 2^{32}$$

The Modular Adder shows up twice here, once for T_1 and once for T_2. Without it, these equations are just abstract bullshit, floating in the void. With it, they're hard-hitting, computational dynamite.

The Erotica of the Modular Adder: Bitwise Fuckery at Its Finest

Oh, baby, let's talk about what the Modular Adder really does to your qubits. Imagine two quantum registers, a and b, each one a pristine collection of qubits in superposition. Then the Modular Adder shows up, cracking its knuckles, and says, "Time to get dirty."

It starts with the carries, entangling qubits in a way that's equal parts elegant and depraved. Each carry bit is a whisper, a promise of things to come. Then comes the addition itself, where the qubits of a and b are combined in a swirling, chaotic dance of controlled gates and quantum interference.

But the real magic happens at the end, when the Modular Adder cleans up after itself. It doesn't just leave the quantum state in disarray—it carefully uncomputes the carries, restoring the ancilla qubits to their original states and leaving the sum perfectly intact. It's not just addition—it's a goddamn work of art.

Conclusion: The Dirty Truth About Modular Addition

The Modular Adder is the unsung hero of SHA256, the operation that turns chaos into order and makes cryptographic magic possible. It's not flashy, but it doesn't need to be. It's raw, powerful, and absolutely essential. Without it, SHA256 is nothing more than a pile of disconnected operations, a sad little shell of an algorithm.

So next time you see a Modular Adder in your code, don't just skim over it. Take a moment to appreciate its beauty, its power, its filthy fucking elegance. Because without this little bastard, none of this would work.

SHA256 Rounds
SHA256 Rounds:

```
def sha256_round(qc, a, b, c, d, e, f, g, h, k, w, n):
    s1 = sigma_1(e, n)
    ch = ch_gate(qc, e, f, g, ancilla)
    t1 = modular_adder(qc, h, s1, ancilla, n)
    t1 = modular_adder(qc, t1, ch, ancilla, n)
    t1 = modular_adder(qc, t1, k, ancilla, n)
    t1 = modular_adder(qc, t1, w, ancilla, n)

    s0 = sigma_0(a, n)
    maj = maj_gate(qc, a, b, c, ancilla)
    t2 = modular_adder(qc, s0, maj, ancilla, n)

    h = g
    g = f
    f = e
    e = modular_adder(qc, d, t1, e, n)
```

```
17    d = c
18    c = b
19    b = a
20    a = modular_adder(qc, t1, t2, a, n)
```

Commentary on SHA256 Rounds

SHA256 Rounds: Fuck me sideways, this is where the algorithm bares its teeth and shows you what it's made of. If you thought the earlier parts of SHA256 were hardcore—rotations, shifts, XORs—then buckle the fuck up, because the rounds take that raw, chaotic energy and crank it to eleven. This isn't just a series of transformations; it's a 64-round quantum bacchanalia where data gets whipped, twisted, and slammed into submission.

Each round is a goddamn spectacle, a dirty tango of modular addition, boolean logic, and relentless state updates that rip through your input like a horny tornado. By the end, the original data is so mangled, so ravaged, it's unrecognizable—transformed into a cryptographic monstrosity that no one can reverse-engineer. And that's the point. This isn't just math; it's a violent, unrelenting fucking of entropy itself.

The Anatomy of a Round: A Fucking Orgy of Operations

Each round is like a carefully choreographed scene in some unholy quantum porno. Here's the play-by-play:

$$T_1 = h + \Sigma_1(e) + \text{Ch}(e, f, g) + K_t + W_t \quad \text{mod } 2^{32}$$

$$T_2 = \Sigma_0(a) + \text{Maj}(a, b, c) \quad \text{mod } 2^{32}$$

$$h = g, \quad g = f, \quad f = e, \quad e = d + T_1 \quad \text{mod } 2^{32}$$

$$d = c, \quad c = b, \quad b = a, \quad a = T_1 + T_2 \quad \text{mod } 2^{32}$$

Every single operation in these equations is a depraved act of cryptographic brilliance, designed to obliterate order and replace it with perfectly chaotic security. Let's break it down, piece by filthy piece.

T_1 : *TheChaoticEngine*

This is the wild, unpredictable heart of the round, where the real entropy magic happens. It combines:

- $\Sigma_1(e)$: A nonlinear mix of rotations and XORs that twists the bits of e into a mess of delicious chaos.

- $\text{Ch}(e, f, g)$: The "choice" function, a sadistic bastard that decides, bit by bit, whether to take f or g, based on the value of e. It's defined as:

$$\text{Ch}(e, f, g) = (e \wedge f) \oplus (\neg e \wedge g)$$

  This isn't logic—it's fucking witchcraft, flipping bits like they're participants in some cryptographic swingers' party.

- K_t: The round constant. A new one for every round, adding a little extra spice to keep attackers guessing.

- W_t: The current message schedule word, freshly mutated from earlier stages to ensure nothing stays the same.

By the time T_1 is done, the data is writhing in a state of pure entropy, begging for more.

T_2 : *TheCounterbalance*

While T_1 fucks everything sideways, T_2 steps in to keep the chaos under control. It combines:

- $\Sigma_0(a)$: Another rotation-XOR beast, but this one's focused on the a variable, twisting it into something barely recognizable.

- $\text{Maj}(a, b, c)$: The "majority" function, defined as:

$$\text{Maj}(a, b, c) = (a \wedge b) \oplus (a \wedge c) \oplus (b \wedge c)$$

  It's like the responsible adult in this cryptographic orgy, ensuring that some semblance of order remains.

Together, T_1 and T_2 are the ultimate power couple—one driving the entropy, the other keeping it from spiraling completely out of control. It's a violent, passionate dance that leaves no bit untouched.

Quantum Implementation: A Goddamn Nightmare of Logic Gates

Now let's talk about the quantum version of this shitshow. Implementing SHA256 rounds in a quantum circuit is like trying to build a cathedral during an earthquake. Every operation—addition, rotation, XOR—requires a symphony of quantum gates, each one carefully choreographed to avoid collapsing the quantum state.

- **Boolean Functions:** The choice (Ch) and majority (Maj) functions are implemented using controlled NOT (CNOT) and Toffoli gates. For example, $Ch(e, f, g)$ involves a series of controlled operations that entangle qubits in ways that would make a classical programmer cry.

- **Sigma Functions:** Rotations are achieved using qubit swaps and controlled gates, carefully moving bits around while preserving the quantum state.

- **Modular Addition:** The biggest pain in the ass. This involves generating carries, propagating them, and then uncomputing them to keep everything reversible.

- **State Updates:** The cascading updates of a, b, c, d, e, f, g, h are straightforward in classical computing but require a goddamn ballet of quantum operations here.

Every step is a challenge, but when it all comes together? Holy fuck, it's beautiful.

The Erotica of SHA256 Rounds: Data Gets Absolutely Wrecked

Picture your input data as a shy, innocent binary string, untouched and orderly. Then SHA256 rounds show up—64 of them—each one more depraved than the last. The data gets rotated, shifted, XORed, and modularly added, over and over, until there's nothing left of its original form. By the end, it's unrecognizable—transformed into a cryptographic masterpiece, dripping with entropy and impossible to reverse.

This isn't just computation; it's fucking art.

Conclusion: The Violent Beauty of SHA256 Rounds

The SHA256 rounds are a goddamn masterpiece of cryptographic engineering. They're brutal, unrelenting, and absolutely essential. Without them, SHA256 would be nothing more than a sad, limp excuse for a hash function.

So next time you're working with SHA256, take a moment to appreciate the rounds. They're not just math—they're fucking magic, turning data into chaos and chaos into security. And isn't that what we're all here for?

Oracle Integration

Oracle Integration:

```
def sha256_oracle(qc, message, target, flag, n=32):
    W = [QuantumRegister(n) for _ in range(64)]
    generate_message_schedule(qc, W, n)

    a, b, c, d, e, f, g, h = [QuantumRegister(n) for _ in range

    for i in range(64):
        sha256_round(qc, a, b, c, d, e, f, g, h, K[i], W[i],

    hash_output = [a, b, c, d, e, f, g, h]
    compare_hash(qc, hash_output, target, flag)
```

Commentary on Oracle Integration

Oracle Integration: Holy motherfucking quantum hell, this is where the SHA256 oracle stops being a theoretical wet dream and slaps its dirty logic right onto the qubits. You've seen the pieces—modular addition, boolean functions, rotations, shifts—but the oracle is the depraved maestro pulling it all together into one gloriously chaotic symphony. It doesn't just compute; it seduces, bends, and mangles your quantum register into submission. This is where quantum mechanics stops whispering and starts screaming.

The oracle isn't just some pedestrian function. No, it's the goddamn ringleader of Grover's algorithm—a black-box dominatrix that slams your data against the problem space and flips a target qubit if, and only if, your input matches the condition. This is the quantum computation equivalent of a filthy, all-night bender: messy, unpredictable, and fucking magnificent.

What the Fuck is an Oracle?

Let's not kid ourselves—an oracle is nothing short of quantum black magic. It's defined as:

$$U_f \left|x\right\rangle \left|y\right\rangle = \left|x\right\rangle \left|y \oplus f(x)\right\rangle$$

Where:

- $\left|x\right\rangle$ is the input—your sacrificial lamb to the oracle's unholy altar.

- $\left|y\right\rangle$ is the target qubit, the one that gets flipped when the oracle's condition is satisfied. Think of it as the oracle's red-light signal for success.

- $f(x)$ is the condition, the mathematical kink that determines whether x satisfies the oracle's twisted desires.

In plain fucking English: the oracle tests whether x is the magic key to the problem and flips $\left|y\right\rangle$ if it is. If not, it leaves the qubits untouched, simmering in their superpositional uncertainty.

Building the SHA256 Oracle: Quantum Torture at Its Finest

Creating a SHA256 oracle isn't just hard—it's a masochistic masterpiece of logical fuckery. Here's how it's done:

1. **Message Schedule Expansion** The first step is to expand the message schedule, turning the input into a sprawling, convoluted mess of mutated words. This involves:

$$W_t = \begin{cases} M_t & \text{for } t < 16 \\ \sigma_1(W_{t-2}) + W_{t-7} + \sigma_0(W_{t-15}) + W_{t-16} & \text{for } t \geq 16 \end{cases}$$

Where:

- $\sigma_0(x) = \text{ROTR}(x, 7) \oplus \text{ROTR}(x, 18) \oplus (x \gg 3)$

- $\sigma_1(x) = \text{ROTR}(x, 17) \oplus \text{ROTR}(x, 19) \oplus (x \gg 10)$

Every one of these operations must be implemented with quantum gates—rotations, XORs, and modular addition—entangling the qubits in a horrifyingly beautiful display of quantum mechanics.

2. **State Transformation** Once the message schedule is ready, the state variables (a, b, c, d, e, f, g, h) are fed through 64 rounds of cryptographic

debauchery. Modular additions, boolean functions, and round constants take turns ravaging the data, leaving no qubit untouched.

3. **Condition Evaluation** The final act is the oracle's pièce de résistance: checking if the resulting hash matches the target. This requires a comparator circuit—a relentless machine that holds the output hash against the target and flips the oracle qubit if there's a match. It's brutal. It's necessary. It's fucking art.

Quantum Implementation: A Glorious Mess of Gates

Implementing the SHA256 oracle on a quantum computer is a Herculean task—a labyrinthine network of gates, each one more intricate than the last. Here's what it takes:

- **Message Schedule Expansion** This step is a clusterfuck of rotations, shifts, and modular addition. Each message word W_t requires controlled NOT (CNOT) gates, Toffoli gates, and ancillary qubits. By the end, your quantum register looks like a battlefield of tangled entanglement.

- **State Updates** The state variables are updated in a cascade of reversible arithmetic. Modular additions are painstakingly implemented, generating and uncomputing carries to maintain coherence. This is quantum computing's version of cleaning up after a wild party—necessary, but exhausting.

- **Output Comparison** The comparator circuit is the oracle's final test. It checks the output hash bit by bit against the target, flipping the oracle qubit if all bits match. This involves controlled operations that entangle the output register with the oracle qubit, ensuring the comparison is quantum-accurate and reversibly filthy.

The Erotica of Oracle Integration: Qubits on Fire

Let's not pretend this isn't sexy as hell. Imagine your quantum register—a pristine array of qubits, untouched and shimmering with superposition. Then the oracle shows up, leather-clad and wielding gates like a dominatrix with a vendetta.

First, it drags the input through the message schedule, twisting and contorting the qubits into a writhing mass of rotations and XORs. By the time the schedule is complete, the qubits are entangled in ways that defy reason and scream, "More!"

Next, the state transformation takes over, slamming the qubits through round after round of modular additions and boolean logic. Each operation builds on the last, driving the entropy higher and higher until the quantum state is teetering on the edge of collapse.

Finally, the comparator circuit delivers the finishing blow. It holds the resulting hash up to the target, entangling the oracle qubit with the output and flipping it if there's a match. It's the ultimate quantum climax—a perfect moment of entangled certainty in an ocean of chaos.

Conclusion: The Oracle as a Dirty, Brilliant Masterpiece

The SHA256 oracle isn't just a function; it's a fucking triumph of cryptographic engineering. It takes the raw, chaotic potential of quantum computing and molds it into a tool of unparalleled power. Without it, Grover's algorithm is just a theory. With it, you've got a quantum wrecking ball, smashing through hash functions like a goddamn legend.

So next time you see an oracle in action, don't just admire it. Worship it. Because this isn't just computation—it's quantum fucking art.

Testing and Simulation

Testing and Simulation:

```
backend = Aer.get_backend('qasm_simulator')
qc = QuantumCircuit(512 + 256 + 1)  # Message, target, flag
result = execute(qc, backend, shots=1).result()
print(result.get_counts())
```

Testing and Simulation

Testing and Simulation: Sweet quantum Jesus on a bicycle, this is where the rubber meets the goddamn road. All the chaos, all the filth, all the profane brilliance of the SHA256 oracle and Grover's algorithm comes down to this: testing the bastard to see if it actually works. It's not just computation anymore—it's a full-blown trial by fire, slamming your quantum circuit into a simulator and watching it scream.

This is the unholy union of theory and practice. You've spent countless hours building the oracle, fine-tuning your quantum gates, and entangling your qubits into a frothy quantum mess. Now it's time to run the damn thing and see if it delivers the goods—or if it collapses into a smoldering heap of quantum failure.

The Setup: Quantum Circuit Fuckery

Let's dissect the Python code driving this simulation, because holy hell, there's a lot going on here.

```
backend = Aer.get_backend('qasm_simulator')
qc = QuantumCircuit(512 + 256 + 1)  # Message, target, flag
result = execute(qc, backend, shots=1).result()
print(result.get_counts())
```

This snippet is deceptively simple, but don't let that fool you—it's the tip of a quantum iceberg that's ready to wreck your classical Titanic. Here's what's happening:

1. **Backend Selection** `backend = Aer.get_backend('qasm_simulator')` This line selects the QASM simulator as the backend for running the quantum circuit. Think of it as the digital dungeon master, orchestrating the entire simulation and making sure every gate, every qubit, and every operation plays out exactly as intended.

2. **Circuit Initialization** `qc = QuantumCircuit(512 + 256 + 1)` Here's where the quantum circuit gets initialized. The parameters—512 for the message, 256 for the target, and 1 for the flag qubit—set the stage for this computational fuckfest. This isn't just a circuit; it's a goddamn battlefield, with qubits lined up and ready to do battle.

3. **Execution** `result = execute(qc, backend, shots=1).result()` This is the moment of truth. The circuit gets executed on the simulator, running a single shot to test its behavior. It's like sending your quantum creation into the wild to see if it survives—or if it gets torn apart by the merciless jaws of simulation errors.

4. **Result Extraction** `print(result.get_counts())` Finally, the results are extracted and printed. The output is a histogram of measurement outcomes, showing the quantum states that emerged victorious from the simulation.

The Chaos of Testing: Will It Fucking Work?

Testing a quantum circuit isn't just about running the code and hoping for the best. No, it's a brutal, soul-crushing process of trial and error, debugging every goddamn gate and tweaking every parameter until the circuit behaves. Here are some of the delightful horrors you'll encounter:

1. **Noise and Decoherence** Quantum simulators don't have to deal with noise, but real quantum hardware? Oh, baby, that's a whole different ballgame. Qubits are finicky little bastards, prone to losing coherence at the worst possible moment. Every gate, every operation, every goddamn microsecond is a battle against the forces of entropy.

2. **Circuit Depth** The more gates you add, the more likely your circuit is to fall apart. This is especially true for monstrosities like the SHA256 oracle, which require hundreds—if not thousands—of gates to implement. Running this thing on actual hardware is like trying to juggle flaming chainsaws in a hurricane.

3. **Measurement Errors** Even in simulation, measurement errors can creep in, skewing your results and leaving you questioning your life choices. One wrong bit in the output can send you spiraling into an existential crisis.

Quantum Erotica: Watching the Circuit Perform

Let's be honest: there's something undeniably sexy about watching a quantum circuit come to life. The way the qubits dance through entanglement, the way the gates weave their chaotic magic—it's like quantum porn for the computationally inclined.

Picture it: your circuit, pristine and untested, takes its first steps into the simulator. The backend fires up, executing each gate with ruthless precision. Rotations, shifts, XORs—all the dirty tricks you've spent hours building come together in a swirling, entangled symphony of quantum fuckery. By the time the results come out, you're left breathless, staring at the raw power of what you've created.

Interpreting the Results: Is It All Worth It?

The output of the simulation is a histogram, showing the measured states of the quantum register. If everything works, you'll see a spike at the state corresponding to the preimage of the hash function. If not, well, it's back to the drawing board.

But let's be real: the first run almost never works. Testing is a painful, iterative process of debugging, tweaking, and rerunning until the circuit behaves. It's not glamorous, but when it finally works? Oh, baby, it's better than sex.

Conclusion: Testing as a Quantum Rite of Passage

Testing and simulation aren't just technical steps—they're a goddamn rite of passage. It's the moment where theory meets practice, where your quantum creation either proves its worth or collapses in shame. It's messy, it's painful, and it's absolutely fucking essential.

So don't skimp on testing. Embrace the chaos, revel in the frustration, and remember: every failed run brings you one step closer to quantum fucking perfection.

Complete Algorithm

Data: 512-bit message input and 256-bit target hash
Result: SHA256 oracle for use in Grover's algorithm

```python
from qiskit import QuantumCircuit, Aer, execute
from qiskit.circuit.library import MCXGate
from qiskit.visualization import plot_histogram
import numpy as np

def xor_gate(qc, a, b, target):
    qc.cx(a, target)
    qc.cx(b, target)

def rotate_right(qc, reg, k, n):
    for i in range(n):
        qc.cx(reg[i], reg[(i + k) % n])

def shift_right(qc, reg, k, n):
    for i in range(n - k):
        qc.cx(reg[i], reg[i + k])
    for i in range(n - k, n):
        qc.reset(reg[i])  # Clear shifted-out bits

def sigma_0(qc, x, result, n):
    rotr_7 = QuantumRegister(n, "rotr_7")
    rotr_18 = QuantumRegister(n, "rotr_18")
    shr_3 = QuantumRegister(n, "shr_3")

    rotate_right(qc, x, 7, n)
    rotate_right(qc, x, 18, n)
```

```python
    shift_right(qc, x, 3, n)

    xor_gate(qc, rotr_7, rotr_18, result)
    xor_gate(qc, result, shr_3, result)

def sigma_1(qc, x, result, n):
    rotr_17 = QuantumRegister(n, "rotr_17")
    rotr_19 = QuantumRegister(n, "rotr_19")
    shr_10 = QuantumRegister(n, "shr_10")

    rotate_right(qc, x, 17, n)
    rotate_right(qc, x, 19, n)
    shift_right(qc, x, 10, n)

    xor_gate(qc, rotr_17, rotr_19, result)
    xor_gate(qc, result, shr_10, result)

def modular_adder(qc, a, b, result, n):
    carry = QuantumRegister(n, "carry")  # Extra qubits for
    for i in range(n):
        qc.ccx(a[i], b[i], carry[i])    # Generate carry
        qc.cx(a[i], result[i])           # Sum bit
        qc.cx(b[i], result[i])           # Sum bit
        if i < n - 1:
            qc.cx(carry[i], carry[i + 1])
    qc.cx(carry[n - 1], result[n - 1])  # Handle final overf

def sha256_round(qc, a, b, c, d, e, f, g, h, k, w, n):
    s1 = sigma_1(e, n)
    ch = ch_gate(qc, e, f, g, ancilla)
    t1 = modular_adder(qc, h, s1, ancilla, n)
    t1 = modular_adder(qc, t1, ch, ancilla, n)
    t1 = modular_adder(qc, t1, k, ancilla, n)
    t1 = modular_adder(qc, t1, w, ancilla, n)

    s0 = sigma_0(a, n)
    maj = maj_gate(qc, a, b, c, ancilla)
    t2 = modular_adder(qc, s0, maj, ancilla, n)
```

```
    h = g
    g = f
    f = e
    e = modular_adder(qc, d, t1, e, n)
    d = c
    c = b
    b = a
    a = modular_adder(qc, t1, t2, a, n)

def sha256_oracle(qc, message, target, flag, n=32):
    W = [QuantumRegister(n) for _ in range(64)]
    generate_message_schedule(qc, W, n)

    a, b, c, d, e, f, g, h = [QuantumRegister(n) for _ in range

    for i in range(64):
        sha256_round(qc, a, b, c, d, e, f, g, h, K[i], W[i],

    hash_output = [a, b, c, d, e, f, g, h]
    compare_hash(qc, hash_output, target, flag)

backend = Aer.get_backend('qasm_simulator')
qc = QuantumCircuit(512 + 256 + 1)  # Message, target, flag
result = execute(qc, backend, shots=1).result()
print(result.get_counts())
```

Index

algorithm, 2

backend, 34
bit, 34

circuit, 34
code, 2
collapse, 32
counterpart, 15
crisis, 34

document, 2
dungeon, 34

edge, 32
elegance, 2
entropy, 26, 32

flair, 15
fucking, 9
function, 9

gate, 34

heart, 26
histogram, 34

implementation, 2
input, 30

life, 34
line, 34

logic, 31

magic, 26
master, 34
measurement, 34
mess, 30
message, 30

nonsense, 15

on, 31, 32
operation, 31, 34
oracle, 2
output, 34

precision, 2

quantum, 32, 34
qubit, 34

right, 14, 15
round, 26, 31

schedule, 30
simulation, 34
simulator, 34
state, 31, 32
step, 30

transformation, 31

wild, 26

Milton Keynes UK
Ingram Content Group UK Ltd.
UKHW021101031224
452078UK00010B/709